My Healthy Body

SKIN, HAIR
AND HYGIENE

Jen Green

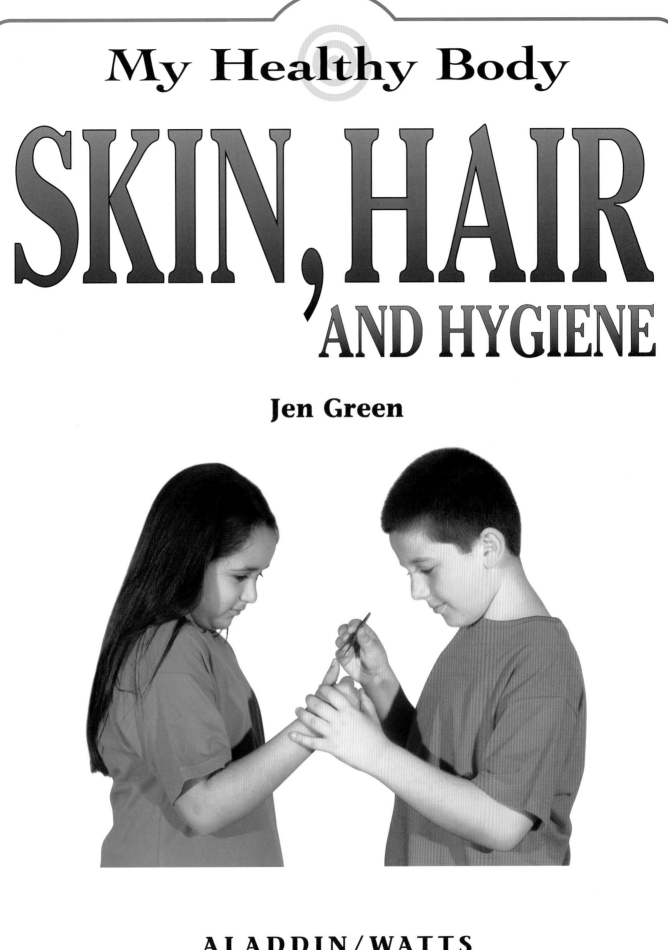

ALADDIN/WATTS
LONDON • SYDNEY

© Aladdin Books Ltd 2003

Produced by:
Aladdin Books Ltd
28 Percy Street
London W1T 2BZ

ISBN 0–7496–5112–1

First published in
Great Britain in 2003 by:
Franklin Watts
96 Leonard Street
London
EC2A 4XD

Editor:
Harriet Brown

Designers:
Flick, Book Design & Graphics
Simon Morse

Illustrators:
Aziz A. Khan, Simon Morse,
Rob Shone, Sarah Smith,
Ian Thompson

Certain illustrations have
appeared in earlier books
created by Aladdin Books.

Printed in UAE
All rights reserved

A CIP catalogue record for
this book is available from
the British Library.

Medical editor:
Dr Hilary Pinnock

Dr Pinnock is a GP working in
Whitstable, Kent. She has written and
consulted on a wide variety of medical
publications for all ages.

Contents

Introduction

What part of your body protects you from germs and injury, keeps you cool in summer and warm in winter? What protective layer that you are wearing is always changing, yet always stays the same? The answer is your amazing skin, which forms a body system with your hair and nails. Read on to find out more about how these parts work and how to keep them clean and healthy through good hygiene.

Medical topics

Use the red boxes to find out about different medical conditions and the effects that they can have on the human body.

You and your skin, hair and hygiene

Use the green boxes to find out how you can help improve your general health and keep your skin, hair and nails in tiptop condition.

The yellow section

Find out how the inside of your body works by following the illustrations on yellow backgrounds.

Health facts and health tips

Look for the yellow boxes to find out more about the different parts of your body and how they work. These boxes also give you tips on how to keep yourself really healthy.

Your skin and hair

The rhino's skin is among the toughest of any mammal. Its fierce-looking horn is made of tightly-packed hair.

Skin forms a protective layer that covers you head to toe. Your skin is breathable, waterproof and washable. Skin even repairs itself when it gets cut. Human skin and hair form a tough barrier, but most animals have even tougher protection. Most mammals are covered in hair or fur. Birds have a thick coat of feathers. Fish (right) and reptiles have scaly skin, and insects have a hard outer shell.

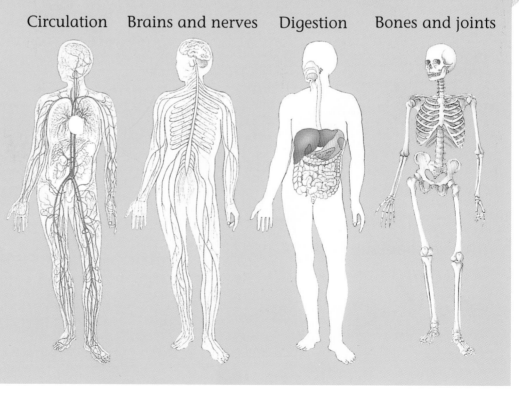

Skin, hair and nails

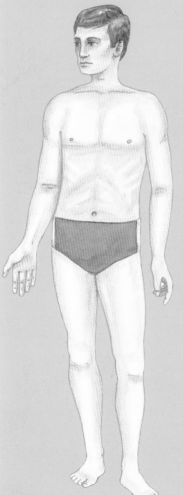

Systems of the body

The circulatory system supplies skin, hair and nails with blood containing oxygen from the respiratory system, and nourishment from the digestive system. Nerves in the skin relay messages to and from the brain.

Circulation   Brains and nerves   Digestion   Bones and joints

4

Your skin

Did you know that skin is the largest, heaviest organ in your body? It's bigger than it looks to cover all the curves and creases in your shape. If spread out, your skin would cover an area the size of an office desk. Skin, hair and nails all contain a tough substance called keratin. The same material forms a bird's claws and a horse's hooves.

Hygiene

In the course of daily life, your body naturally gets sweaty, dirty, and also smelly. But dirt may contain germs that can make you ill, and body smells caused by stale sweat and a dirty body are off-putting. Help yourself stay healthy through good hygiene – by washing regularly with soap and water.

Your hair

You have two types of hair on your body: a layer of fine hairs all over, and the coarser hair on your head, eyebrows and lashes. The palms of your hands and soles of your feet are among the few parts that have no hair.

What use are skin and hair?

Your eyelashes shield your eyes from dust. Your eyebrows can be used to show feelings such as delight, anger and surprise.

Skin and hair have many different functions that help keep your body running smoothly. Skin forms a waterproof layer that keeps the outside world out, and body fluids and the rest of your insides in! It also helps to control your body temperature. Skin provides you with a sense of touch, so you can detect heat, cold, pain and pressure. Skin and hair shield you from injury and the Sun's harmful rays.

Fingernails and toenails
Nails prevent the really sensitive parts of fingers and toes from cuts. They are made from tough keratin, like your hair. Healthy nails look pink. This means that they have a good blood supply.

Temperature control
Skin plays a vital role in keeping your body at an average 37°C. In hot weather, your skin flushes and you sweat to lose heat. In cool weather, your skin turns pale and you shiver to save heat (see pages 10-11). Hair also helps to keep you warm.

Waterproof barrier

Oily sebum, made by sebaceous glands in your skin, lubricates your skin and keeps it waterproof. Skin also acts as a barrier that makes sure your internal organs don't dry out.

Dirty nails
Dirt and germs lurk under fingernails. If germs get into your mouth, they can make you ill. So keep nails scrubbed, and trim them regularly to stop them getting too long.

Helpful hair

The hair on your head provides cushioning that helps to protect you from knocks. Together with your skull, it helps shield your delicate brain from injury.

Sun protection

Skin and hair provide some protection from harmful ultra-violet (UV) rays in sunlight. Skin can be damaged by too much sunlight, so it's important to wear sunscreen.

Defence against infection

Your skin is the first line of defence against germs – microscopic bacteria and viruses that are everywhere, and can cause infection. Washing removes germs and dirt. Germs can enter your body through cuts in your skin, which is why it's important to clean all wounds thoroughly (see pages 14-15).

Protect yourself from infection by washing your hands regularly (above) and by cleaning any cuts or grazes (left).

Skin up-close

You may be surprised to know that skin is one of the most complicated organs in the body. There are two main layers. The top layer, the epidermis, is made up of dead cells that are always flaking off. The living layer below, called the dermis, contains blood vessels, sweat glands, nerves, and hairs in deep pits called follicles. Under your skin is a layer of fat.

Every day, you shed millions of dead skin cells as you move about. Don't worry, dead skin cells are constantly replaced with new, living cells!

Skin thickness

Most of your skin is about 1 mm thick. The skin on your eyelids and lips is thinner – only about 0.5 mm thick. The skin on the soles of your feet is thickest because it gets a lot of wear and tear.

Arm skin

Older cells

New cells

Foot skin

Older cells

New cells

Epidermis

Dermis

Nerve

Sweat gland

Sebaceous gland

Follicle

Hair root

Skin layers

Your skin is about 30 cells deep. The epidermis consists of hard, flat cells that overlap like roof tiles. As these are gradually shed, cells from the base of the epidermis move up to replace them. It takes about three weeks for a new skin cell to reach the surface. As cells move up, they are filled with keratin, which makes them germ- and waterproof.

Fingerprints

The skin on your fingertips is raised in tiny ridges that are arranged in patterns. Whenever you touch a smooth surface, your fingers leave an oily print. No two fingerprints are the same, which is why they can be used to solve crimes. Compare your fingerprints with those of your friends.

Blood vessels

Toughened skin

If a patch of skin gets rubbed away regularly, it protects itself by growing thick and tough. Workers who use their hands or feet (below left and right) for rough work, develop hard patches of skin called calluses. People who regularly go barefoot can develop hard skin up to 5 mm thick on the soles of their feet.

Wear gloves to protect your hands when doing rough work. Wear shoes that fit well and are suitable for the activity you're doing.

Temperature control

In cold weather, your muscles shiver to generate heat. Like the other responses described here, shivering is beyond your control.

Like all mammals, humans are warm-blooded, which means our body temperature stays the same whatever the outside conditions. Your skin plays a key role in keeping your body at an even 37°C. It responds to hot conditions by sweating and flushing red, which helps to avoid overheating. Shivering and goosebumps help you to keep warm when it is cold.

Sweating
In hot conditions, glands in your skin give off sweat, which escapes through holes called pores. As sweat evaporates it cools you down.

Losing heat

When you're hot, blood vessels in your skin get wider. This allows more warm blood to flow near the surface, which cools it down. The skin in areas such as your face becomes pink and flushed.

Heat and body hair
In hot weather, the fine hairs all over your body lie flatter against your skin. This helps to keep you cool.

Blood vessels

Head hair and warmth

You lose more body heat through your head than through any other part of your body. The thick hair on your head traps air to reduce the amount of heat that escapes in this way. Wearing a hat in cold weather also helps you to keep warm.

Frostbite

In sub-zero temperatures, blood vessels in exposed parts of the body may close down to reduce blood flow and prevent heat from escaping. This may cause the surrounding tissues to freeze – a condition called frostbite. Fingers, toes and ear lobes are the areas most often affected by frostbite.

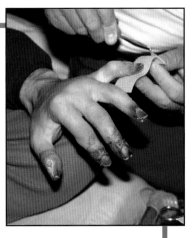

Muscle

Keeping warm

In cold weather, blood vessels in your skin narrow to reduce the amount of blood flowing near the surface. Muscles pull your body hairs upright, trapping a layer of air next to your skin. This helps to warm you.

After exercise

Exercise makes you hot and sweaty. As soon as you finish exercise, put on extra clothing to avoid getting chilled. Sweat becomes smelly as it dries. Always wash thoroughly after exercise, paying special attention to areas that get extra-sweaty, such as your armpits, groin and feet.

11

Skin problems and allergies

Sleeping is good for your skin! Too little sleep gives you bags under your eyes. Infections such as cold sores flare up if you get overtired.

Spots are a common skin problem affecting young people and some adults. Spots are most likely to erupt during teenage years. Due to hormone changes taking place in the body at this time, the skin can become particularly oily. In time, spots become less of a problem as skin becomes less oily again. Medication prescribed by a doctor may control the spots. It is also believed that using some foods and herbal remedies can help to control spots and other skin problems.

Acne

Acne is the name given to the rash of red spots that is common among teenagers. These spots can erupt when hair follicles – the pits in your skin from which hairs grow – get blocked by grease and dirt.

Skin allergies

Many materials can cause sensitive skin to react badly. For example, you may get an allergic reaction after touching animal fur, certain plants or skin creams. The skin erupts in an itchy rash. Some foods can cause a similar reaction. Avoid materials or foods that make your skin react badly.

1. A spot starts when a hair follicle gets clogged by oily sebum produced by your skin.

2. As the greasy area attracts dirt, a dark, waxy plug called a blackhead forms.

3. Sometimes the blocked pore becomes inflamed, and the spot gets larger and more painful.

Eczema

Eczema is a skin inflammation which most commonly affects the hands, face, back of the knees and inside of the elbows. The skin becomes dry and flaky and very itchy. It may start to bleed if you scratch it. Special cream prescribed by your doctor can help control the problem.

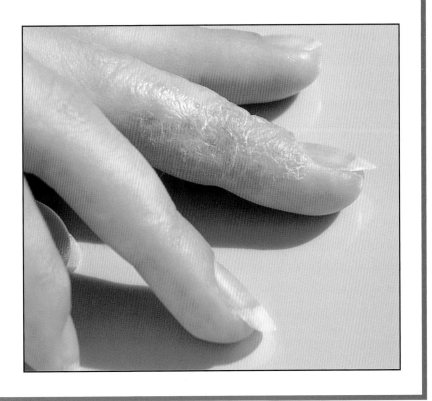

Stings

Bee and wasp stings cause soreness and swelling. If the sting is left in, gently remove it with tweezers. Wash the wound and apply a cold, damp cloth. Get medical help if the victim is allergic to stings or has been stung on the mouth or throat.

Rashes

Illnesses such as measles, mumps and chickenpox cause the skin to erupt in a rash. This reaction is part of the illness and dies down naturally as you recover. Avoid scratching the spots as they may become infected or leave permanent scars.

Skin hygiene

The best way to look after skin is to keep it clean. It's especially important to cleanse skin after wearing make-up. Don't squeeze spots – it only makes them worse, by spreading the inflammation. Remove grease by giving your face a brisk wash and then gently towel it dry.

13

Skin and healing

Your skin has the amazing ability to repair itself from injuries such as cuts, bruises and grazes. Skin and blood act together to seal the wound by clotting, and forming a scab while the damaged area heals. When the skin is fully healed the scab drops off, leaving little trace of the injury. A scar may remain after a deep wound or if the scab is removed before a cut is healed.

Bruising is caused by blood leaking under the skin after a blow. A black eye looks dramatic but fades in 10-14 days.

(1)

Cut through skin

Blood vessel

Cuts and grazes

When you cut yourself, germs can enter through the break in your skin and cause infection. That's why it's important to wash cuts and grazes thoroughly, then put a clean plaster over the wound.

Clotted blood

(2)

Fibrin strand

Red blood cells

Platelets

White blood cell

Scab

(3)

How cuts heal

When skin is cut (1), tiny blood cells called platelets gather and stick together to form a clot (2). Blood then produces fine strands of a protein called fibrin, which seals the gap with a scab (3). White blood cells kill off any germs.

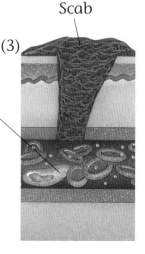

Cuts and splinters

Cuts should be washed to remove any dirt. Apply an antiseptic to kill germs and put a plaster over the wound to keep out dirt. To remove a splinter from the skin, notice how the splinter went in and gently pull it out at the same angle using tweezers. Don't touch an open cut on someone else unless you're wearing rubber gloves.

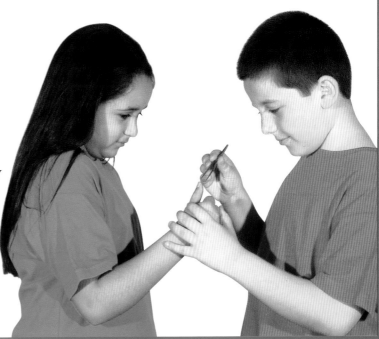

Burns and scalds

Treat burns and scalds by holding the injured area under cold water. Then cover the wound with a clean bandage. Serious burns need hospital treatment.

Skin grafts

If a large area of skin is badly burned or otherwise injured, doctors may use skin taken from another part of the person's body to patch the injury. This is called a skin graft. Artificial skin is sometimes used instead.

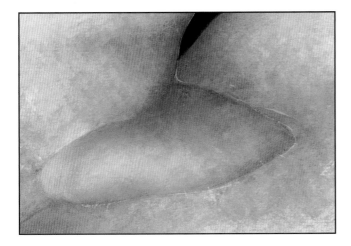

Foods for scars

Vitamins found in fruit, vegetables, dairy products, wheatgerm and eggs help scars to heal more quickly. It is important to eat a balanced diet to keep your skin healthy.

Stitches

Deep cuts or gaping wounds need to be stitched by a nurse or doctor. The stitches pull the sides of the wound together while the injury heals. Later, most stitches have to be taken out. Steristrips are special plasters that are also used to hold a cut together while it heals (right).

15

Skin and the Sun

Protect yourself from harmful UV rays by wearing a hat and T-shirt, and using sunscreen when you spend time outdoors.

Skin can be damaged by rays from the Sun called ultraviolet (UV) rays. A dark pigment (colour) called melanin helps to protect your skin from the sunlight. Melanin is made by special star-shaped cells called melanocytes, found between the dermis and epidermis. Sunlight causes the melanocytes to release more dark pigment grains, which then spread out through the skin to tan it. General skin colour is also caused by melanin.

Skin colour

People from various parts of the world have different skin colours because of differing levels of melanin in their skin. Pale skins contain relatively low levels of the protective pigment, dark skins have the most.

Asian skin
People originally from Asian countries have moderate levels of melanin in their skin. Their skin is darker than that of people from cold places, but paler than African skin.

White skin
People originally from cool countries have pale skin because they do not need so much protection from weaker sunlight.

Black skin
People originally from hot, sunny countries such as parts of Africa have high levels of protective melanin, so their skin is dark.

Harmful effects of sunlight

Too much sunlight damages your skin and can burn you, causing soreness and making the skin peel. Long exposure to sunlight causes the skin to wrinkle, which makes people who spend too much time in the Sun look older (above). UV rays can also cause skin cancer.

Moles

Moles are areas of skin that contain extra melanin. Moles are common and usually harmless. If a mole is often itchy, gets larger or bleeds, it should be checked by a doctor.

Seasonal affective disorder

People who feel depressed in winter may be suffering from Seasonal Affective Disorder (SAD). Lack of light in winter can result in high levels of a chemical called melatonin, which is thought to cause SAD.

Benefits of sunlight

A moderate amount of sunlight is good for you because it makes your skin produce an important vitamin, vitamin D. However, the Sun's rays can damage your eyes, so never look at the Sun directly. Good sunglasses can protect your eyes against the glare of the Sun.

Ozone hole

A layer of ozone gas high in the atmosphere shields us from UV radiation. The use of chemicals called CFCs has made this layer thinner, particularly near the poles. Ozone loss above the South Pole is shown in this false-colour photo. This has now increased the risk of skin cancer, so it's extremely important to use sunscreen.

Your sensitive skin

Skin provides you with the sense of touch, which is one of the body's main senses. Your skin contains a variety of sensors which detect heat, cold, pressure, vibration, pain and other sensations. Being able to sense pain plays an important role in keeping you safe.

Sitting still for a long time can squash nerves and make a part of your body feel numb. You get 'pins and needles' in your skin as it recovers from the numbness.

Nerve endings that detect light pressure

Free nerve endings

Nerve endings

Tiny sensors and nerve endings at different levels in your skin are specialised to detect various sensations. Some nerves detect light pressures such as the touch of a feather. Other nerve endings at deeper levels in the dermis detect stronger pressure, such as a pinch. Free nerve endings detect heat, cold and also pain.

Nerve endings that detect harder pressure

Extra-sensitive
Some areas of skin are more sensitive than others because they contain more nerve endings of certain kinds. In this cartoon, the most sensitive areas are enlarged. The most sensitive parts are your lips, the palms of your hands and the soles of your feet.

18

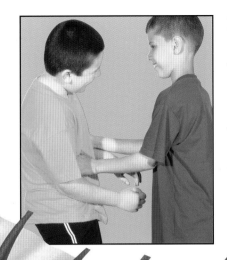

How ticklish are you?

Some people are more ticklish than others. Touch-sensitive areas such as the soles of feet are easier to tickle than parts with fewer nerve endings, such as your arms. Use a feather to find the sensitive parts of a friend's body!

Reflexes

If you prick your finger, nerve endings in the skin send a message to your brain to warn of danger. Before the signal reaches the brain, the spinal cord tells your muscles to jerk your hand away from the pain source. This reflex action helps keep you safe.

Acupuncture

Acupuncture is a form of Eastern medicine that uses needles to ease pain and heal illness. It involves pricking the skin at key points on the body. In China, doctors have used acupuncture for 3,000 years. It is now widely used in Western countries, too.

Sensing and numbing pain

Pain is a vital early warning system. It tells you that part of your body is being injured, so that you can act to prevent further harm. However, it is often useful to numb pain. Pain-killing drugs of various kinds prevent pain signals from reaching the brain.

19

Good hygiene

Sweating helps to keep your body temperature even, both when you are active and at rest, but stale sweat soon gets smelly. Regular washing is vital if you want to smell nice and feel fresh. Good hygiene is especially important after exercise and before eating. Use warm water, soap, a nailbrush and a sponge or flannel to remove the grime of daily life. Your clothes get dirty and smelly along with the rest of you, so it's important to wash them too.

Oily sebum builds up in hair that isn't washed regularly, making it greasy and dirty. Treat your hair to a shampoo every few days.

Germs and hygiene

Your skin is home to millions of microscopic life-forms. Most of these are harmless, but some cause disease. Always wash hands after you go to the toilet, touch an animal or do dirty work such as gardening. If germs get into food they can make you ill, so give hands a scrub before you eat.

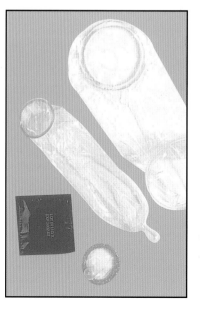

Sexually-transmitted diseases
Diseases and infections such as pubic lice, herpes and HIV are spread by sexual contact. People having sex use protection such as condoms to avoid catching sexually-transmitted diseases. This helps them to stay fresh and healthy.

Teeth care

When you eat, food gets stuck in your teeth. Sugar and bacteria work to cover teeth with an acidic layer called plaque and to create cavities. Twice-daily brushing helps gets rid of food and plaque and keeps teeth and gums healthy.

Cavity

Germs and surgery

Before the 19th century, no one knew that germs cause infection and illness. Operations took place in unhygienic conditions. The importance of hygiene was then discovered, and germ-killing measures were introduced. Caps, masks, gowns and gloves are now worn in operations to avoid spreading germs.

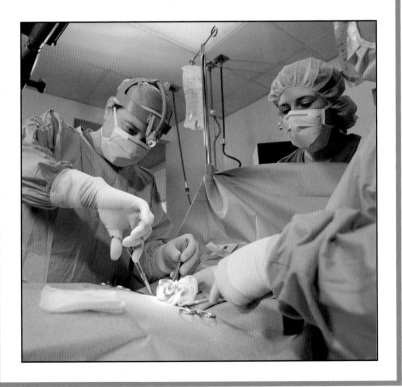

Mentally fresh

Stay mentally alert by taking regular exercise. Swimming, dancing and all kinds of sport increase the level of oxygen reaching your brain. This sharpens your responses and makes you feel keen and alert!

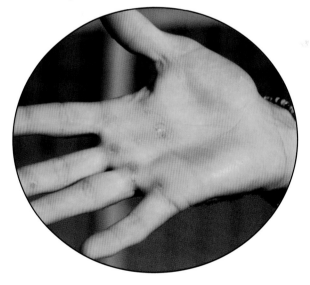

Blisters and skin infections

Skin develops painful blisters when it is rubbed, for example, by badly-fitting shoes. Use a plaster to protect the sore skin. Athlete's foot and verrucas are common skin infections. Washing feet and drying carefully between the toes, cuts down your risk of catching these infections.

All about hair

Of the five million or so hairs on your body 10,000 are on your scalp. Hairs are made of tough keratin, like animal horns and claws. Close-up (below right), you can see that the scales of keratin on the surface overlap like roof tiles. This makes hair strong.

Head hair normally grows to about 1 m if you don't cut it. The record for hair length is over 4 m long!

Hair growth

Hairs are made of thin, flattened strands of cells. A hair grows from the root, where cells multiply, lengthening the strand and pushing it out of the follicle.

Hair up-close

The whole length of hair that you see is dead – only the root is alive! The sebaceous gland produces sebum to make the hair shiny. Blood vessels supply the root with oxygen and nourishment. The arrector muscle pulls the hair upright to trap air when you are cold.

Sebaceous gland

Arrector muscle

Blood vessels

Hair follicle

Root of the hair

Hair colour

Hair colour is caused by melanin, the same pigment that colours your skin. One type of melanin is dark-brown, another type is reddish. The proportion of each pigment in your hair produces many different colours, from black and brown to red and blonde.

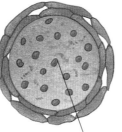

Pigment

Common colours

Hair colour is an inherited trait, passed down from parents to children. Make a chart to record the hair colour of everyone in your class. What is the most common colour? Which is the least common colour?

Hair and puberty

When you are young, you only have coarse hair on your head, eyebrows and lashes. At puberty as you begin to become an adult, hair grows in your armpits and around your genitals. In men, hair also grows on the cheeks, chin and top lip, and thicker body hair grows on the chest, arms and legs.

Number of people

8
7
6
5
4
3
2
1

Colour   Black   Red   Blonde   Brown

Type of hair

Is your hair straight, wavy or curly? The type of hair you have depends on the shape of the follicle openings from which hairs grow. Is it fine or thick? Thickness depends on whether follicles are small or large. Thick hair grows from large follicles, fine hair from small.

Straight hair grows from follicles with round openings.

Oval follicles produce wavy hair.

Curly hair grows from follicles with narrow, rectangular openings.

Looking after hair and nails

Like skin, your hair and nails benefit from regular cleaning. Shampooing hair every day or so removes dirt, oil, sweat and dead cells, and leaves hair glossy and squeaky-clean! Scrub nails regularly, and trim them with scissors or clippers. The best time to trim nails is after a bath or shower, when they are soft.

Like hair, nails are made of dead cells filled with keratin. The longest nail ever recorded was a thumbnail 102 cm long!

Greasy and dry hair

Glands at hair roots release oily sebum to give hair its shine. Too much sebum produces greasy hair. Solve this by frequent washing. If the glands produce too little oil, hair becomes dry. Using a mild shampoo and conditioner can help.

Ingrowing toenails

Shoes that are too tight can squeeze toes, causing toenails to cut into the surrounding flesh. This causes painful ingrowing toenails. A chiropodist (foot expert) can trim the misshapen nail. Cut toenails straight, not curved, to avoid this problem.

Close-up of a split end

Split ends
Regular wear and tear or frequent use of hair dye and other chemicals can produce rough, brittle hair with ragged 'split ends'. Trimming the ends will sort the problem out, while still leaving hair as long as you choose.

Nails

The nails that protect your toes and fingers grow from the root continuously. Along the nail bed, they are cushioned by a pad of flesh. Biting your nails can cause infection, and doesn't look cool. Try just keeping one nail to bite and allow the rest to grow.

Nail root
Nail bed
Finger bone

Hair and nail care

Daily brushing or combing leaves your hair silky, shiny and free of tangles. Wash combs and brushes regularly in warm, soapy water.

Sharing combs or brushes can spread infections such as head lice (below). Chemicals in nail varnish remover can make nails brittle. If your nail splits, cut it off carefully.

Tangles and dandruff

Start brushing tangled hair near the ends, then work towards the roots. Using conditioner will help. Dandruff is an infection that causes the skin of the scalp to flake. Use a medicated shampoo to solve the problem.

Head lice

Lice are tiny insects that live in hair and lay their eggs there. These pesky insects jump from one head to another, but a special shampoo will kill them. The eggs can be combed out with a very fine comb.

Skin and hair through life

Your skin and hair slowly change as you get older. Hair that is lush when you are young may change colour and thin with age. Skin all over the body is elastic when you're young. As you grow older, it gets less flexible and wrinkles form. Taking care of skin and hair helps you look good throughout life.

Unlike flexible human skin, a snake's scaly skin cannot stretch as it grows. The old, too-tight skin is shed, to reveal a slightly bigger skin beneath.

Skin and aging
Pinch the skin on your arm, and it springs back to shape. Fibres of an elastic material called collagen make your skin supple. As you get older, the collagen becomes less stretchy, so wrinkles appear.

Hair through life

Most people's hair slowly changes colour and texture as they get older. Babies often have very fine hair, which later becomes thicker. After the age of 25, hair may become thinner as fewer hairs grow to replace worn-out hairs that drop out.

Hair in old age
Later in life, hair produces less of the melanin pigment that colours it, so people start to go grey. Hair that produces no pigment looks grey or white.

Children's hair
Babies and young children often have very fair, blonde-white hair, which gradually darkens with age.

Stretch marks

A pregnant woman's belly swells as the unborn child inside her grows. Stretch marks often form on the stretching skin. These never disappear but they do fade over time. Rapidly-growing teenagers may also develop stretch marks.

Baldness

You shed around 80 head hairs every day, but new hairs normally replace them. As you get older, fewer hairs grow to replace the lost ones. The head may gradually become bald. This affects more men than women.

Varicose veins

Varicose veins sometimes affect older people. Veins running beneath the skin on the legs swell, to produce bulges. This condition can be made worse following pregnancy and by spending too much time standing. Exercise and avoiding sitting with your legs crossed at the knee is thought to help prevent varicose veins.

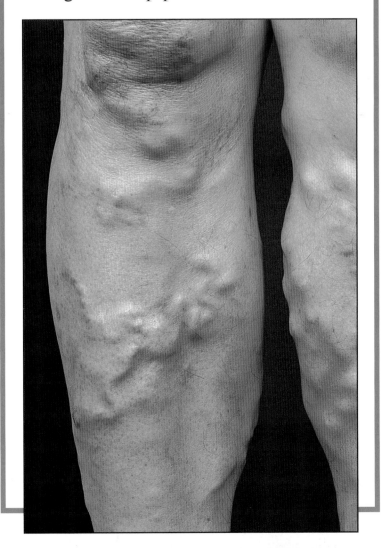

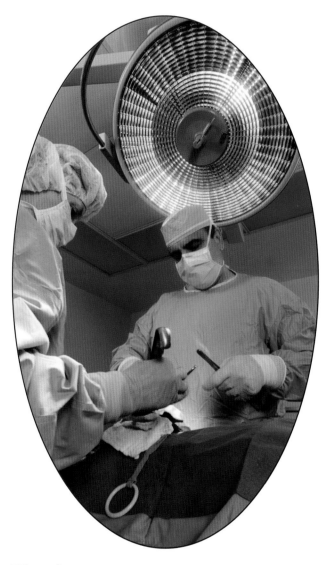

Plastic surgery

Adults sometimes pay for a form of plastic surgery called a 'facelift'. The surgeon cuts out a section of skin, and stretches the remaining skin to smooth away wrinkles. But most people feel that wrinkles are a natural part of growing old.

Keeping healthy

Skin, hair, nails and teeth are the main parts of your body that are visible. So if your skin and hair are looking good, you are looking good! Skin is also one of your body's main defences against germs and infection. It makes sense to look after your skin and hair through good hygiene, eating the right foods, taking regular exercise and getting enough sleep.

Getting your hair trimmed every 6-8 weeks helps to keep it healthy. Otherwise, your hair may split and look tatty.

Feeding skin, hair and teeth

The old saying "You are what you eat" is true! A balanced diet with plenty of fresh fruit and vegetables supplies the protein, vitamins, minerals and fibre you need for healthy skin and hair. Too much fatty or sugary food such as chips, cakes and sweets are bad for skin and teeth. Crunchy foods such as apples and carrots are much better. Drinking lots of water every day is important, too.

Body art
People have tattooed and pierced their bodies for thousands of years. Both processes puncture your skin so only a qualified person should do the job. Tattooing is painful and can only be removed by surgery. There are lots of temporary tattoos that are fun to use.

Glove protection

Rubber gloves protect hands when you are washing up. Some sports, such as cycling and horse riding, can cause your hands to blister, so wear gloves.

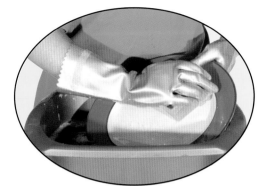

Staying clean

As you get older, sweat glands in your armpits, groin and feet start to work harder. It becomes even more important to wash daily, and wear clean underwear. When girls start their periods, they need to take special care with hygiene.

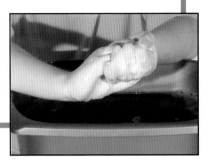

Exercise

Aerobic exercise brings a glow to your skin, as your heart and lungs work hard to pump oxygen to your muscles. Playing sport or activities such as swimming or dancing three times weekly helps to keep your skin and hair in top condition.

Sleep

Your skin and hair reflect your general state of health. Dull skin and hair may be a sign that you need more sleep and fresh air. Sleep enables the body and mind to re-energize, repair and to keep healthy.

Amazing facts

An adult's skin weighs up to 4 kg and would cover 2 square metres if spread out. Skin is made up of about 3 million skin cells!

The 'house dust' that gathers in the corners of our homes is mostly dead skin that has flaked off our bodies. Dust mites like to feed on this dust!

Dust mite

Fingernails grow about 1 mm in a week. That's about four times faster than toenails.

Some babies are born with silky hair called lanugo on their bodies. This hair is usually shed before they are born.

Hair grows at a rate of about 1 mm every three days, and about 1.2 cm every month.

Glossary

Acne A rash of red pimples produced by over-oily skin.

Aerobic exercise Any type of moderately strenuous exercise which causes the heart and lungs to work harder, pumping oxygen-rich blood to the muscles.

Allergic reaction When the body's immune system reacts to a harmless substance as if it were dangerous.

Callus A patch of toughened skin produced by rubbing. Protective calluses form on parts of the body that get extra wear.

Dermis The lower layer of skin, which contains blood vessels, nerves, sweat glands and the roots of hairs.

Epidermis The upper layer of skin, made up of dead skin cells that gradually flake off.

Follicle A pit in the skin from which a hair grows, enclosed by a tube of skin.

Keratin A body protein that strengthens human skin, hair and nails.

Melanin A dark pigment (colour) found in skin, which tans the surface to protect you from the Sun. Hair also contains melanin, which gives it colour.

Melanocyte A star-shaped cell found in the skin, which releases grains of melanin to tan the skin.

Ozone layer A layer of gas high in Earth's atmosphere that filters out harmful ultraviolet rays from the Sun.

Platelets The tiny cells in blood that help blood to clot.

Pore An opening in the skin through which sweat escapes.

Sebaceous gland A gland found in the dermis that produces sebum, an oil which lubricates hair.

Sweat A salty liquid produced by glands deep in the skin, which evaporates when it reaches the surface to cool you down.

Ultraviolet rays Radiation produced by the Sun that can cause skin to burn and peel, and may trigger skin cancer.

Index

Photocredits

Abbreviations: l-left, r-right, b-bottom, t-top, c-centre, m-middle

All photos supplied by PBD except for: 3br, 5tl, 7b, 12mr, 19tr, 20bm, 23b all, 26br, 27tr, 30mt, 30bl – Roger Vlitos. 4tr, 6mr, 26ml, 26bl, 30c – Digital Stock. 7ml, 21tr, 26cr, 29mr – Digital Vision. 7tr, 11br, 17mr, 20mr, 21bl, 27mr – Corbis. 9mr, 9bm, 15mrt, 15c, 17tl, 26mr – Corel. 11tr – Jason Burke/Eye Ubiquitous/Corbis. 13tr – Sheila Terry/Science Photo Library. 15mrb – Stockbyte. 17br – NASA. 19mr – Oscar Burrel/Latin Stock/Science Photo Library. 21mr – Nik Wheeler/CORBIS. 24ml – Dr P Marazzi/Science Photo Library. 26cl – Brand X Pictures. 27bl – Alex Bartel/Science Photo Library.